Cows Have Calves

by Lynn M. Stone

Animals and Their Young

Content Adviser: Terrence E. Young Jr., M.Ed., M.L.S.
Jefferson Parish (La.) Public Schools

Reading Adviser: Dr. Linda D. Labbo,
Department of Reading Education, College of Education,
The University of Georgia

COMPASS POINT BOOKS

Minneapolis, Minnesota

Compass Point Books
3722 West 50th Street, #115
Minneapolis, MN 55410

For more information about Compass Point Books, e-mail your request to:
custserv@compasspointbooks.com

Photographs ©: Lynn M. Stone, Pictor/Les Moore, 20.

Editors: E. Russell Primm and Emily J. Dolbear
Photo Researcher: Svetlana Zhurkina
Photo Selector: Linda S. Koutris
Design: Bradfordesign, Inc.

Library of Congress Cataloging-in-Publication Data

Stone, Lynn M.
    Cows have calves / by Lynn Stone.
        p. cm. — (Animals and their young)
    Includes bibliographical references and index.
    Summary: An introduction to the life cycle of cattle from birth to adult, discussing appearance, food, instinct,
and nurturing.
    ISBN 0-7565-0001-X (lib. bdg.)
        1. Calves—Juvenile literature. [1. Cows. 2. Cattle. 3. Animals—Infancy.] I. Title. II. Series: Stone,
Lynn M. Animals and their young.
SF205 .S76 2000
636.2'07—dc21   00-008831

Table of Contents

What Are Calves?

Calves are the babies of **cows** and **bulls**. Female cattle are called cows. Male cattle are called bulls. Farmers raise some cattle for their meat. Farmers raise dairy cattle for their milk. This book is about calves born to dairy cattle.

◀ A cow takes care of her calf.

How Do Calves Arrive?

A calf is born about nine months after a cow mates with a bull. It can be born at any time of the year. A dairy cow usually has one calf at a time, but she could have twins. It is unusual for a cow to have three calves at one time.

Less than an hour or two after birth, a calf can take a few wobbly steps. A calf needs to stand to reach its mother's **udder** and suck her milk.

Young calves drink milk from their mother's udder.

How Do Calves Feed?

A calf is born with the **instinct** to suck milk from its mother. It knows what to do right away without being taught.

Dairy farmers usually put a mother cow back in the milking barn within a day of the birth. People drink most of the cow's milk. The newborn calf sucks its mother's milk from a bottle. Calves fed by bottles drink about 1 gallon (4 liters) of milk each day. Calves that **nurse**, or feed from their mother, may drink more.

◀ This calf drinks from a bottle.

What Do Newborn Calves Do?

A newborn calf can see, hear, and smell things. It is tired but not helpless.

The newborn calves nap often. But they quickly become more active. Soon they jump and run around. They often kick and bump each other in calf pens.

A newborn calf naps near its mother.

What Does a Calf Look Like?

A newborn calf looks just like its mother. Of course, a calf is much smaller than its mother. It weighs about 90 pounds (41 kilograms). The size of the calf depends on the kind, or breed, of its mother and father.

Like its mother, a calf has a rounded, wet nose. It has its mother's big, dark eyes. Like its mother, it has a coat of thick hair to keep it warm. It even moos like its mother!

A calf has long skinny legs. But the calf will soon grow and its body will match its legs.

Young calves are much smaller than their parents.

What Colors Are Calves?

If a calf's parents are both the same color, the calf is usually that color. If the parents are not the same color, the calf may look like either one. Or it may be a mixture of colors.

Most dairy calves in North America have black-and-white coats. They are from a breed called Holsteins.

◀ This black-and-white cow and calf are Holsteins.

What Do Young Calves Do and Eat?

A calf spends all its time with other calves. They eat, sleep, and run together in pens or sometimes in grassy fields.

After eight weeks, the calves are no longer given milk. When calves are **weaned**, they stop drinking milk from their mother or from a bottle. They drink water and eat about 6 pounds (3 kilograms) of dry food every day. Their food is called calf starter. It is made of corn, oats, sweet molasses, and fresh alfalfa hay.

◀ After eight weeks, young calves don't drink their mother's milk.

What Happens As a Calf Grows Older?

As a calf grows older, it eats more hay and less calf starter. Some one-year-old calves graze on grass in the fields. But the dairy farmer still gives them extra food.

Older calves spend most of their time eating and then chewing their **cud**. Cattle bring food from their stomachs back into their mouths to chew again. This food is called cud.

◀ A row of calves feed together on the farm.

When Is a Calf Grown Up?

A **heifer** is a female calf. On her first birthday, a heifer weighs between 600 and 800 pounds (272 and 363 kilograms). The heifer will not reach her full size for two or three years. But now she is old enough and big enough to have calves of her own.

A heifer becomes a cow when she has her first calf. She may live to be eight or nine and have a calf every year. But she probably won't give birth to more than four calves in her lifetime.

◄ A heifer is called a cow when she has her first calf.

Glossary

bull—an adult male cow; a father cow

cow—an adult female cow; a mother cow

cud—swallowed food returned to the mouth from the cow's stomach for more chewing

heifer—a young cow that has not yet had a calf

instinct—knowing what to do without being taught

nurse—drink mother's milk

udder—the baglike part under a cow's belly where milk is made

weaned—taken off mother's milk and given solid food

Did You Know?

- A dairy cow gives about 256 glasses of milk a day.

- In one year, a dairy cow gives 14,460 pounds (6,640 kilograms) of milk.

- There are more than 1.3 billion cows in the world.

Want to Know More?

At the Library

Cole, Joanna. *A Calf Is Born*. New York: Morrow, 1975.

Kaizuki, Kiyonori, and Cathy Hirano (translator). *A Calf Is Born*. New York: Orchard Books, 1990.

Ling, Mary. *Calf*. New York: Dorling Kindersley, 1993.

On the Web

Cows of the World

http://www.tc.umn.edu/~puk/cow/cowworld.html

For information about the more than 900 cattle breeds from around the world

Straus Family Creamery: Kid's Page

http://www.strausmilk.com/kids.htm

For information about milking cows and making butter

Through the Mail

National Dairy Council

10255 West Higgins Road

Suite 900

Rosemont, IL 60018-5616

For information about milk and its important role in people's diets

On the Road

Visit your county fair in the late summer or ask your parents or teachers to check for tours of your local dairy.

Index

About the Author

Lynn M. Stone has written hundreds of children's books and many articles on natural history for various magazines. He has photographed wildlife and domestic animals on all seven continents for such magazines as *National Geographic, Time, Ranger Rick, Natural History, Field and Stream*, and *Audubon*.

Lynn Stone earned a bachelor's degree at Aurora University in Illinois and a master's degree at Northern Illinois University. He taught in the West Aurora schools for several years before becoming a writer-photographer full-time. He lives with his wife and daughter in Batavia, Illinois.